AMAZING
ESCAPES

Thomas G. Gunning

AMAZING ESCAPES

Illustrated with photographs and prints

DODD, MEAD & COMPANY • *New York*

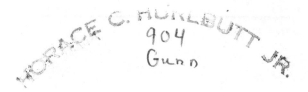
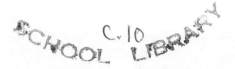

Copyright © 1984 by Thomas G. Gunning
All rights reserved
No part of this book may be reproduced in any form
without permission in writing from the publisher
Distributed in Canada by
McClelland and Stewart Limited, Toronto
Manufactured in the United States of America

2   3   4   5   6   7   8   9   10

Library of Congress Cataloging in Publication Data

Gunning, Thomas G.
  Amazing escapes.

  Includes index.
  Summary: Presents nine tales of escape and survival
against great odds including escapes from a great white
shark, a volcanic eruption, and a fall through a thunderstorm.
  1. Escapes—Juvenile literature. 2. Adventure and
adventurers—Juvenile literature. 3. Survival (after airplane accidents, shipwrecks, etc.)—Juvenile literature.
[1. Survival. 2. Escapes. 3. Adventure and adventurers]
I. Title.
G525.G85   1984   904   83-25401
ISBN 0-396-08324-2

904
Gunn
C·10
8.95

To Joan, my wife and best friend

CONTENTS

INTRODUCTION

Between the covers of this book are stories of nine escapes. Some stories tell of escapes from danger. Other stories tell of escapes to freedom.

Luck played a part in some of these escapes. But courage, daring, a burning desire to stay alive and live free played far more important parts.

Some of the escapers were soldiers, who are expected to be brave in time of danger. Others were just plain everyday people. Somehow, all of them were able to reach down deep into themselves and find whatever was needed to escape.

1

ESCAPE FROM A GREAT WHITE SHARK

Not many people have come face to face with a great white shark and lived to tell about it. A great white shark is a huge beast and will attack anything—fish, whales, people, and even boats. It seems more like an evil machine than a creature of the deep. But there's one man who was carried off in the killer jaws of a great white shark and somehow escaped with his life. He is Rodney Fox of Australia, and in case you don't believe him, he's got the scars to prove it.

On a sunny day during the summer of 1963, Rodney grabbed his skin-diving equipment, waved good-bye to his young wife, and headed down to the beach. It was the day of the Skin-diving and Spear-fishing Contest. The idea of the contest was to spear as many fish as you could in five hours. The winner would be the person who had the heaviest load of fish and the most different kinds of fish.

Two years before, Rodney had won the contest, and last year he had come in second. This year he was in his best shape ever. And he aimed to win. He was quitting this year and he wanted to go out on top.

Rodney had a good day. He speared fish after fish. Shortly before the contest was to end, he figured he needed a few more fish. He wanted to get some big ones, so he moved fairly far from shore. There, about 20 feet underwater, he spotted a fish that weighed about 20 pounds. Moving through the water as quietly as he could, Rodney lined up the fish with his spear gun. But he never got a chance to shoot the spear. Something grabbed him by the left foot. Now it

11

had him around the chest and back. Suddenly Rodney was being pushed through the water like a runaway submarine. His spear gun had been torn from his hands. His face mask had been ripped from his head. Being face down in the water, Rodney couldn't see who or what had a hold on him. He tried to pull away, but the thing had too tight a grip on him. With a sickening feeling, Rodney suddenly realized what was holding onto him. He was caught in the jaws of a shark.

The giant killer shark was tearing through the water carrying Rodney Fox in its huge jaws. It all seemed pretty hopeless. But Rodney Fox wasn't about to give up without a fight. Reaching behind his back, he tried to jam his fingers into the shark's eyes.

It must have worked. The giant jaws opened up, but the danger was far from over. While trying to get away, Rodney's hand and arm slipped into the shark's mouth. The

A great white shark slipped up behind Rodney Fox and grabbed him with its killer jaws.

shark closed its jaws. Somehow, Rodney was able to pull his hand out, but his arm was badly cut. And then pain hit Rodney like a bolt of lightning. He thought he was going to pass out.

With pain shooting through his body and lungs aching for air, Rodney struggled to the surface. The shark immediately came up after Rodney, so he didn't even get a chance to call out for help. To keep away from the shark's slashing jaws, he climbed onto its rough back. Rodney took a deep breath as the shark dived. The monster shot through the water. Although Rodney's right arm was almost useless, he was able to hang on.

Rodney was soon out of air, so he kicked free and rose to the surface once more. Seconds later, the ugly head of the great white shark appeared just a few feet away. The shark was coming at him. Its mouth was open. Rodney could clearly see its rows of three-inch teeth. "This is the end," Rodney thought to himself. Amazingly, though, the shark passed right on by!

Rodney got away from the shark. But it went after him again.

For a few seconds, Rodney thought the danger was over, but it wasn't. Suddenly, Rodney was tearing through the water again. The shark had grabbed Rodney's float. Inside the float was a place where fish he caught could be kept. The float was attached by a long line to Rodney's belt. Now the monster was pulling the float and Rodney along with it. Rodney had a new fear. He had escaped the jaws of death, but now he was afraid he was going to drown. He tried to

15

undo his belt, but with his badly cut arm that was impossible. Just as Rodney was about to pass out, the rope snapped and he swam to the surface.

Most of the skin on Rodney's right arm was gone. He had huge teeth marks across his chest and back. And he had left a trail of blood in the water. Luckily, Rodney had a thick rubber wet suit on, or else his wounds would have been worse.

As soon as he hit the surface, Rodney cried out, "Shark! Shark!" The other skin divers hurried to his side. Seeing how badly he was hurt, they rushed Rodney to the hospital. It took a team of doctors and nurses four hours to sew up Rodney Fox.

Rodney Fox now has long, ugly scars on his chest and back, and, for a while, his right arm and hand were hard to use. Still, he was lucky. The great white shark had only grabbed him with its teeth and held him. For some unknown reason, the shark didn't chew him up. With its giant teeth and jaws, the beast could have bitten him in two.

With its giant jaws and huge teeth, the great white shark could have killed Rodney Fox. The photographer who took this picture was saved by the bars of his underwater cage.

Rodney doesn't enter diving contests anymore. He just dives for fun. But he's more careful now. He doesn't go off by himself. He doesn't go out too far. And he doesn't carry bloody fish around. That's just asking for trouble. Sharks can smell a drop of blood in the water hundreds of yards away.

Years after his attack, Rodney helped some scientists. They had spent much of their lives studying killer sharks. But in talking with Rodney they have learned a lot. The scientists were trying to find out more about shark attacks. And if there's one person who knows about shark attacks, it's Rodney Fox. After all, he's been as close to a shark attack as you can get.

2

UP, UP, AND AWAY

A few years ago, eight people from East Germany made one of the most daring escape attempts of all time. In a way, the nearly 17 million people who live in East Germany are prisoners. After World War II, which ended in 1945, Germany was divided into East and West. In time, East Germany became a Communist country. In West Germany, the people had more to say in the government. Some three million people in East Germany fled to West Germany. There was freedom in the West. And there were more jobs and higher pay. But in 1961, the

East German government told its people they couldn't leave.

Along the border between the two countries high fences with sharp metal tops were put up. The border between East and West Germany had always been guarded, but now extra soldiers and policemen were added. Even the waterways that the two countries share were carefully watched.

Mines that blow up when stepped on were buried in fields near the border. Machine guns that shoot by themselves when someone comes near were set up. Over the years, close to 200 people have been killed trying to sneak out of East Germany.

Even though it is dangerous, hundreds of people escape from East Germany each year. Some hide in car trunks. Some swim to freedom. One man built a submarine and floated under water to freedom. Another man used his scuba-diving equipment and swam to West Germany. Others have flown to freedom in small planes and gliders.

But no one had used the way of escaping

tried by the Wetzel and Strelzyk families. The Wetzels and Strelzyks were going to flee to the West in a hot-air balloon that they had made in their basements.

Hans-Peter Strelzyk, a 37-year-old airplane mechanic, had gotten the idea some two years earlier. He was watching a TV show about hot-air balloons. He and his friend Guenter Wetzel, a 24-year-old bricklayer, had often talked of making the break for freedom. But it had only been talk. Both men were married and had two children each. How could they possibly get all those people out of East Germany? But now Strelzyk had a plan. What if they built a hot-air balloon and flew to freedom? The balloon could easily carry all eight of them. They would leave late at night and fly silently over the hated fence.

Both families got together and talked over the plan. They figured that it was such a weird way to escape that it just might work.

For the following months, Wetzel and Strelzyk read all they could about hot-air balloons. When they felt they knew enough, they started building the balloon. With the help of Strelzyk's sons, they built a small platform on which the eight people would stand. They also built a burner that would heat the air in the balloon. Since hot air rises, the heated air would carry the balloon up and away. The wives, Doris Strelzyk and Petra Wetzel, started sewing the balloon. They used curtains, sheets, tablecloths, and any other large, thin pieces of cloth they could find.

They sewed very carefully. They knew their lives and the lives of their husbands and children depended on them. If stitches began to rip out at 6,000 feet, it could be the end of all of them.

At last, the balloon was finished. It was 60 feet wide and 75 feet high. Attached to the balloon was the small platform. The sides of the platform were made of ropes tied to

This photo from the movie Night Crossing *shows what the homemade escape balloon looked like.*

metal pipes which had been built into each corner.

On the night of July 3, 1979, the two families sneaked off into the countryside. They took only some warm clothes, their newly built balloon, and four tanks of propane gas for heating the balloon's air. Everything else they left behind—their furniture, their homes, their TVs.

The men filled their balloon with cold air, which was then warmed with the burner. The families began their flight to freedom. At first, everything was fine. Silently the balloon floated toward West Germany, but then it started coming down too soon. The families landed safely. But they were still a few yards inside East Germany's border. They were so close to freedom. Yet at the same time, they were so far. Fearing they would be captured by guards, the families sneaked away. But they had to leave their balloon behind. The balloon was picked up by East German police.

The families decided to try once again. Two months later, on the night of September 15, they again left their homes. They drove to a place called Lobenstein, which is not too far from the border. From there they hoped to fly to Naila, a small town in West Germany.

By about two o'clock in the morning, the balloon was almost ready for lift-off. But then Strelzyk gave the balloon a little too much heat. It started taking off without the families. Strelzyk jumped aboard and yelled to the others to hop on.

Peter and Doris Strelzyk and their children, Frank and Andreas, are sitting on the platform of their hot-air balloon.

The balloon rose quickly. Soon they were some 6,000 feet above the ground. The air was cold but quiet. Suddenly, searchlights lit up the sky. "Please don't shoot," Strelzyk begged silently. "Please don't shoot." The families were in luck. The searchlights failed to pick them up.

The minutes passed. As it neared West Germany, the homemade balloon began to come down. At first it fell slowly. But as the air inside cooled, the balloon fell faster. Then it was just over some treetops. It nicked a tree and thumped down in a field of grass. Luckily, it had missed an electrical wire that was nearby.

Guenter's leg was banged up. And some of the children had cuts on their faces. But no one was badly hurt. Had they made it to freedom? They didn't know. Once again, the balloon had come down before it was supposed to. Just in case they were still in East Germany, they hid.

Carefully, they watched the road. Wetzel spotted a police car. It looked like an East

After their escape, the Strelzyk and Wetzel families flew to the United States to talk about doing a movie of their amazing escape.

27

German police car. But then he noticed the shape of the headlights. The car was an Audi. Audis are made in West Germany. East German police wouldn't have a car made in West Germany. There were shouts of joy as the families rushed out to the road to tell the story of their amazing flight to freedom.

3

JET GETAWAY

Young Frank Jarecki seemed to have everything he wanted. He was a top pilot in the Polish Air Force. Because he was a pilot, he was making good money and had a fine home and plenty of food. He was better off than most of the people in Poland. It was 1953. World War II had been over for eight years. But Poland hadn't gotten back on its feet yet. Many of the people had to dress in old clothes and didn't have enough food to eat.

Still, Jarecki wasn't happy. He felt a little funny when he saw that so many people were thin and ragged, while he was well dressed and had more than enough food. But he didn't feel free in Poland. Poland was ruled by Communists from Russia. The people of Poland had little say about the way their country was run. If you spoke out against the leaders, you might find yourself in prison.

It seemed to Jarecki that he had hated the Russians and the Communists for as long as he could remember. On a cold morning in January of 1940, Russian soldiers had taken Frank and his mother from their home. They were forced to walk through a snowstorm to the railroad station some six miles away. The Jareckis and hundreds of other Polish people were forced into a cattle car. They sat in the crowded car for three days and three nights. There was no food or water. Finally, nine-year-old Frank passed out. Many others died along the way. When he came to in Russia, Frank was questioned closely. The Russians must have figured the nine-year-old was no danger to them. They let him and his mother return to Poland. But aunts and uncles were sent to Siberia, a very cold part of Russia. Frank never saw them again.

As he was growing up, Frank put his hatred of the Russians aside. In time, his mind became filled with a dream. He wanted to fly. Maybe he thought that being high in the sky would be a kind of freedom.

Frank was one of 150 young men chosen to go to pilots' school, which the Russians ran. Some 8,000 men had tried to get in. Once in school, Frank even joined the Communist party. As one of the school's top students, he gave lessons to the others on Communism. He didn't really believe in what he was teaching. But he decided it would help his dream of flying come true. The Russians wouldn't train anyone to be a pilot who didn't go along with their ideas.

Because he was such an outstanding student, Frank was given a radio by the Russian general in charge of the Air Force. Today radios are cheap and easy to get. But in Poland in the 1950s, a radio was almost price-less. Jarecki used his Communist gift to listen to programs put on by the U.S. and England. The programs spoke often of freedom.

Later, Jarecki became the first Polish pilot to fly a Russian MiG. The MiG was Russia's best jet plane. Being chosen to fly one was an honor. But then Frank was quite a pilot. He was so good that a sign was put up at the airfield. The sign said, "Follow the example of Jarecki."

Jarecki enjoyed his flying, but his hatred of the Russians was growing. With the Russians around, there was no trust. Everybody seemed to be spying on everybody else. Frank had been asked to spy on his good friends. And he was sure that some of his friends had been asked to spy on him. With all that spying going on, you couldn't have any real friends.

Finally, it all got to be too much for Jarecki. He would make a break for freedom. He knew it would be dangerous. The Air

Force kept four of its best jets ready at all times to chase and shoot down anyone who tried to escape. Even so, Jarecki knew he had to give it a try.

On March 4 of 1953, word got out that Joseph Stalin, the Russians' leader, was seriously ill. "Now is the time," thought Jarecki. The Russians were upset about Stalin. They weren't watching as carefully as they usually did.

That night Jarecki was given his flying orders for the next day. He and three other pilots would fly along the coast. They would be flying over a town called Kolobrzeg. Kolobrzeg is only 60 miles from Bornholm, an island in the country of Denmark. Jarecki had heard that the United States Air Force had a large airfield on Bornholm. Jarecki would turn at Kolobrzeg and fly as fast as he could to Bornholm. There he would give himself up to the U.S. Air Force. He would also ask for asylum. Asylum means that a country will let a person live there. The country will not send the person back to his own country even if that country wants him or her back.

The next day, March 5, Jarecki took off with the other pilots as usual. He tried to act like nothing was wrong. But he was feeling a bit shaky inside and he felt a kind of sadness, too. After all, if his escape worked, he would never see his mother again or his friends.

A few minutes after takeoff, the planes, flying at 30,00 feet, were over Kolobrzeg. It was now or never. Jarecki radioed the plane in front of him and asked the pilot to move over a bit. That way Jarecki could fly out over the sea and drop his fuel tanks. Without the fuel tanks, the jet would be lighter and fly faster. With a sweating hand, Jarecki tried to push the button that would drop his fuel tanks into the sea. His hand slipped. He tried again. The fuel tanks dropped off.

Seeing the fuel tanks falling from Jarecki's jet, the other pilots knew what was happening. There was no turning back now. Jarecki turned his plane hard left and went into a dive. The jet went screaming toward Born-holm.

On his radio, Jarecki heard one of the pi-lots yelling, "731 is making a getaway!" Back at the air base, a Russian was yelling, "Come back! Come back!."

And then Jarecki heard something that froze the sweat on his body. "Carry out Op-eration Cross!" a voice on the radio said. Operation Cross meant that Jarecki's plane was to be shot down on sight.

Of course, they'd have to catch him first. With his jet going at top speed, Jarecki was over Bornholm in eleven minutes. And then he got a nasty surprise. There was no U.S. airfield on Bornholm. There was just a tiny landing strip. It was only some 4,000 feet long. A jet needed a landing strip or field about 10,000 feet long. Jarecki had made it to Denmark. But he was in very serious dan-ger.

Jarecki circled the field, slowing the plane as much as he dared. Then carefully he touched down. When he reached the end of the runway, he quickly turned his plane around and let it taxi back the way he had come until the jet came to a stop.

Jarecki hopped out of his plane and ran toward a group of people watching him. He waved his hands high in the air. In Polish, he excitedly explained that he had escaped from the Communists and wanted freedom. The Danes did not speak Polish. But they understood why he had come. His face was lit up with the joy of freedom.

The Communists were as angry as they could be. They demanded that Denmark hand over Jarecki. But Denmark said no. Jarecki was given asylum.

Jarecki's mother, though, was put in jail. She had nothing to do with the escape. She didn't even know her son was leaving. Frank thought it was too dangerous to tell her. He figured maybe if she didn't know about the escape the Communists wouldn't punish her. But he figured wrong. She spent three years in jail.

Although the Communists were angry,

Jarecki, in the dark flying suit, is standing near the jet he flew to freedom.

the U.S. was as happy as it could be. The new MiG was a top secret plane. Now the United States Air Force would get its first close-up look at an undamaged MiG.

Later, Frank Jarecki moved to the United

In 1958, Frank Jarecki became a citizen of the United States.

States. He was given a warm welcome. There were parades in New York City, Buffalo, Detroit, and other cities for Jarecki. To the people of the United States, Frank Jarecki was a real-life hero.

But even heroes have to make a living. After going to college, Jarecki got two jobs. By working an extra job, he was able to save enough money to open a machine shop. In time, he became a millionaire.

Life in the United States has been good to Frank Jarecki. He still misses his mother. He can write to her and she can write to him. But he hasn't seen her since 1953 and may never see her again. The Communists will not let Frank's mother visit him. And he will never go back to Poland.

Even so, he's glad he escaped. As he puts it, "If I'd stayed, I'd probably be in jail. They ordered two of us pilots to spy on the others. And I didn't want to do that. I was a good flier but not a spy."

Besides, Frank loves the United States. He says, "Anybody can succeed here if they

Today Jarecki owns a factory that makes parts for machines and is a rich man.

want to work and if they do a good job. This is the greatest country."

4

THE AMAZING BADER

Bader should have known better. As a leader in the British air force, he had often told his men not to attack enemy planes alone. It was just too dangerous. Yet when Bader, while flying over France, saw a half-dozen German fighters, he couldn't help sneaking in behind them.

With a quick burst of gunfire, he hit the lead plane. But then while trying to get away, the back of his plane hit the propeller of one of the enemy planes. Like a flying power saw, the propeller cut off the tail of Bader's fighter. Within seconds, Bader's plane was spinning toward earth.

At first, Bader was too surprised to think clearly. But he soon realized he would have to parachute from the plane. With his strong arms, he lifted himself halfway out of the plane. But then he couldn't move anymore. His foot was stuck. Suddenly, though, Bader felt himself falling through space.

Bader pulled the parachute ring that he had been tightly holding and then watched thankfully as his parachute opened overhead. He still wasn't sure how he had managed to get out of the plane. But then he looked down and saw that his right leg had been pulled off.

For once he was glad that he had artificial legs. Otherwise, caught by the foot in the plane, he would have gone crashing to his death.

Soon after he landed in France, German soldiers picked up Bader and took him to a nearby hospital for prisoners. Germany had beaten France in the early months of World War II. So German soldiers were stationed in many parts of Europe. At the hospital, a surprised German doctor told Bader that he had lost a leg. "Yes," Bader said calmly . "It came off as I was getting out of my airplane." At first, the doctor was shocked. But then he realized that Bader hadn't lost his right leg that day. It had happened a while back. Seconds later, the doctor was again surprised when he discovered that Bader's left leg was also artificial.

Then he understood. He was taking care of Douglas Bader, the famous legless pilot. Everyone had heard of Bader. Even the enemy knew about him.

Later, German pilots came to meet Bader. Although he was on the other side and had shot down more than twenty of their planes, they liked his courage. They also wanted proof that he really was legless. It was hard for them to believe that a man with two artificial legs could fly so well.

Bader asked one of the German officers if he would search through Bader's wrecked plane. Bader wanted the man to see if he

could find the artificial leg that had been torn off. The leg was found, but it was bent. Bader, however, was able to talk the Germans into fixing it.

When the metal leg was returned, fixed and even shined up, Bader was as thankful as could be. "It's really great," Bader told the German officer who brought the leg to him. "It's very good of you to have done this. Will you please thank the men who did it very much indeed?"

Although he was sincerely thankful, a few days later Bader used his fixed-up leg to sneak away from the Germans. With the help of a young Frenchman, Bader managed to walk to a home some ten miles away. There he was hidden by some French citizens. However, he was soon found by the Germans. They were plenty angry. They felt embarrassed that a man with artifical legs had escaped from them.

In the meantime, a spare leg had been par-

Bader was one of England's best fighter pilots.

achuted from a British plane to the Germans. The Germans had told the British that one of Bader's legs had been damaged when his plane crashed. The Germans, however, would not give the spare leg to Bader. In fact, they took both his artificial legs away from him. They also told two heavily armed soldiers to guard him.

Of course, without his legs, Bader was just about helpless. But the Germans were playing it safe. Very safe. There was no telling what a man like Bader would try.

As it turned out, Bader tried time after time to escape, but he never made it. He stayed 215 days as a prisoner of war until April of 1945 when American soldiers set him free.

After the war was over, Bader went to work for an oil company. He flew on his own to dozens of countries around the world. When not working or flying, he spent

When one of Bader's artificial legs was damaged, a new one was made and dropped by parachute.

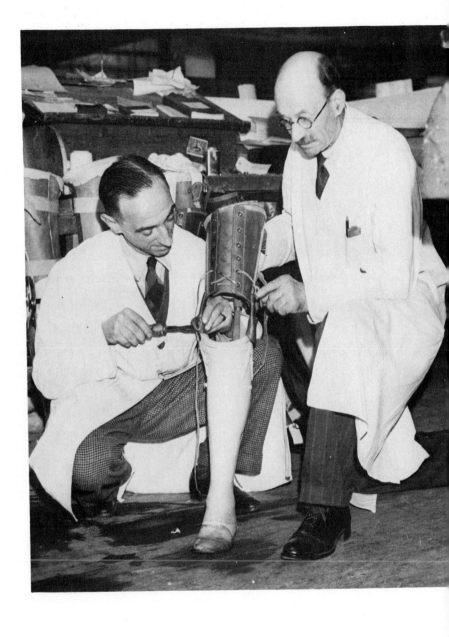

a lot of time playing golf and dancing. Bader also set aside time to talk to others who had lost arms, legs, or hands. Bader told these people that they could lead rich, full lives if they gave it a try. Needless to say, when Bader spoke, they listened. He was walking proof of his words.

Bader talks to a young boy who has lost both his legs and an arm.

5

THE DAY OF DEATH

It was a few minutes before eight on the morning of May 8, 1902. For Auguste Ciparis, a 25-year-old prisoner in the city of St. Pierre, it was time to eat. For just about everyone else in that city of 30,000 people, it was time to die.

St. Pierre, which is on the island of Martinique in the West Indies, is a few miles from Mount Pelée. Pelée is a volcanic mountain. On April 23, 1902, there were some small explosions coming from the volcano. A few days after that, the volcano started shooting ashes high into the sky. The ashes fell on St.

Pierre like dirty snow. Everywhere the people looked there was a thick covering of dust. The dust burned their eyes and throats.

On May 5, the side of the volcano cracked open. Because of heavy rain, a lake of water had formed in the crater or a bowl-like pit in the mouth of the volcano. The water had been brought to a boil by the volcano's gases. The boiling lake burst through the crater's cracked walls. Racing down the volcano's side, the boiling water picked up ash and huge rocks. This heated mud slide rolled over a sugar mill, killing 30 men inside before crashing into the sea.

By this time, the people of St. Pierre were afraid. Hundreds packed up and left. But the people who ran the city said there was nothing to be afraid of. As St. Pierre's newspaper put it, "We cannot understand the panic. Where could one be better off than at St. Pierre?"

Most people believed the newspaper. They stayed. In fact, thousands of people from nearby towns and farms came to St. Pierre because they thought they would be safer there. However, the animals of St. Pierre seemed to know something that the people didn't. By this time, there were no birds around St. Pierre. Even the snakes had left. The animals that couldn't leave were acting very strange. The cows were making funny noises and dogs were howling far into the night.

On the morning of May 8, a tall cloud of gray steam was shooting out of Mount Pelée. There were ashes in the air, but the wind blew these away from St. Pierre. The air over the city was clear. The day was bright and sunny.

Just about eight o'clock, there were four earsplitting explosions. Suddenly the sides of the volcano blew out. One thick cloud of steam and dust shot straight up into the air. A second cloud shot outward, staying close

Smoke pours out of Mount Pelée in this picture taken some years after St. Pierre was destroyed.

to the ground as it raced down the mountain toward St. Pierre.

Within two or three minutes, the boiling hot cloud had swept over the city. Moving with the power of a tornado, the cloud knocked over just about everything that was in its way. Roofs were ripped off and walls were turned into piles of stone. Thick pieces of steel were twisted out of shape. Bits of hot dust from the cloud set thousands of fires. Even the ships tied up at St. Pierre weren't safe. Of the 18 ships that were tied up there, only two escaped. Worst of all, people died on the spot as the hot cloud of death swept over the city. The killer cloud burned the breath right out of their bodies.

Darkness fell on St. Pierre as thick clouds of dust from the volcano hid the sun and covered the burning city. Mixed in with the clouds were pieces of hot rock. And then a heavy rain fell on St. Pierre. The rain and

The man can't believe his eyes as he looks at what the volcano has done to St. Pierre.

dust mixed and the city was soon covered with a dark gray mud. It was just a few minutes after eight o'clock, but St. Pierre was destroyed.

One newspaper, *The New York Times*, said that everyone in St. Pierre had been killed. But the *Times* was wrong. On the morning of May 8, Auguste Ciparis was in an underground jail cell. His cell was really a dungeon and was underneath the city's jail. There were no windows in his cell. There was only a small opening in the top part of the door. Ciparis was waiting for breakfast. Suddenly, it grew very dark. Hot air and ashes poured in through the opening in the door. Ciparis could see no flames or smoke, but his back and legs were badly burned. While the cell was filled with heat, Ciparis fell to the floor and held his breath as long as he could. Soon the heat passed. It was all so strange and sudden. There had

The New York Times *said that the dead may have numbered 25,000. Today it is believed that 30,000 were killed.*

VOLCANO DESTROYS WEST INDIAN TOWN

St. Pierre, Martinique, Entirely Wiped Out.

DEAD MAY NUMBER 25,000

It Is Said that All the Inhabitants of the Town Have Been Killed.

SHIPS IN HARBOR DESTROYED

The News Taken to St. Lucia by a British Steamer, Seventeen of Whose Men Were Killed—Quebec Steamship Company's Vessel Roraima Lost with All on Board.

LONDON TIMES–NEW YORK TIMES
Special Cablegram.

LONDON, May 9.—The correspondent of The Times at St. Thomas, Danish West Indies, states that the town of St. Pierre, in the French Island of Martinique, has been totally destroyed by a volcano.

All the inhabitants of the town, says the correspondent, have lost their lives, and all the shipping in the harbor has been destroyed.

est disaster in the history of the island occurred in 1767, when 1,600 persons were killed by an earthquake. In 1839 the present capital, Fort Royal, was visited by an earthquake which destroyed nearly half the town, damaged the whole island, and killed 700 persons.

From the mountains in the interior of Martinique several ranges of low volcanic hills extend to the sea, and between them lie broad fertile valleys. The principal productions of the island are sugar, coffee, cotton, cassia, bananas, indigo, maize, and ginger. The manufactures possess considerable importance, there being several establishments for the preparation of indigo, about 100 for the various processes in the preparation of sugar, coffee, cocoa, and cotton, besides potteries, lime kilns, and steam mills. There is active commerce, chiefly with France. In 1896 the imports amounted to £915,420 and the exports to £857,241.

The island was seized by the British in 1762, 1781, 1794, and 1809, and was finally restored to France by the treaty of Paris in 1814. Slavery was abolished in 1848, and since 1866 the island has legislated for itself in regard to customs duties and public works.

Martinique is famous as the birthplace of one of the most celebrated women in history, Josephine, first Empress of the French. She was born within a few miles of St. Pierre, on the plantation of her father, M. Tascher de la Pagerie, of an old French Creole family. Here she met her first husband, Vicomte Alexandre de Beauharnais, who had also been born on the island.

He was one of the French who fought in this country under Count de Rochambeau. Beauharnais in 1789 was elected a Deputy to the States General by the nobles of Blois. He was guillotined July 23, 1794, while his wife was in prison, awaiting execution. She was among those released by the fall of Robespierre.

Josephine died at Malmaison while Napoleon was at Elba. A beautiful statue to her was erected by the people of Martinique in one of the squares of St. Pierre. The ruins of the old De la Pagerie plantation were still to be seen a short time ago, and many visitors to the island made a pilgrimage to see the places identified with the childhood of Josephine. It was near St. Pierre that an old negro woman told her when she was a child that she would be Empress of the greatest Empire in the world.

In American naval history St. Pierre will be forever remembered as the place where Cervera's squadron first turned up on this side of the Atlantic after leaving the Cape been no noise or smoke or flames. Even though Ciparis's back was badly burned, his shirt had not caught fire.

In pain and afraid, Ciparis cried out for help. But there was no answer. Still, Ciparis called out every hour or so until he got too weak to yell. After four days, Ciparis heard men talking. "Help! Save me!" Ciparis cried.

Two men, who had come to look over St. Pierre, were surprised to hear a voice. They had been over much of the city. Everywhere they looked there was death. They were sure that everyone had been killed.

Hearing Ciparis's cry for help, they yelled, "Who's that? Where are you?"

"I'm down here!" Ciparis shouted. "Get me out!"

Quickly the two men dug away the rocks and found Auguste Ciparis. Ciparis was weak. But after the two men gave him a drink of water, he was able to walk with them to a town some five miles away.

For a while, it was thought that Ciparis

was the only person in St. Pierre who escaped death. But later, it was learned that a shoemaker who lived in the far end of town had not been killed. But then he had not been in the middle of the blast. And there was a woman in a basement who had stayed alive. But she died a few hours after being found. So out of 30,000 people only two escaped death.

Later, the shoemaker became a guard in St. Pierre. His job was to make sure that people didn't steal anything from the city. Auguste Ciparis was not put back in prison. People believed that he had been through enough. Ciparis got a job with a circus. A prison cell just like the one he had been in was built by the circus carpenters and Ciparis sat there while people looked at him. Over the years, thousands came to see the "Prisoner of St. Pierre." To them, there was something very strange about a man who had escaped death when so many others had been killed.

6

ESCAPE FROM A THUNDERSTORM

They call William Rankin "The Man Who Rode the Thunder." Rankin once parachuted into the middle of a thunderstorm and was held prisoner by it.

It happened on a summer evening back on July 26, 1959. At that time, Rankin was a pilot in the Marines. He and another pilot were flying their single-engine jets from South Carolina to Massachusetts and back again. Except for a few storm clouds, the weather was just about perfect. The return trip should have been an easy 90-minute flight. But over Norfolk, Virginia, Rankin

Rankin was flying a single-engine jet like the one shown in this photo.

heard a thump. Seconds later, one of the jet's emergency lights flashed on. "Fire," the bright red light warned.

Rankin was really worried. A fire is one of the worst things that can happen to a jet. Thinking that maybe the engine was overheated, he slowed the plane down. He hoped this would cool it off. He also radioed to the other pilot and told him he was having engine trouble.

Slowing down the jet worked. The fire warning light went out. But then the engine stopped dead. Rankin knew he had to get out in a hurry or it was all over. Without power, the jet would either fall into a spin that might tear the plane apart or it would rocket to earth. There was only one thing to do: eject. Because jets travel so fast, a pilot just can't jump out of one. He has to be ejected or shot out of the jet.

Reaching up behind him, Rankin grabbed the jet's ejection handles and pulled them forward. A heavy curtain, which was attached to the ejection handles, fell over his eyes. The special curtain would protect his face when the air outside tore at him. A moment later, the jet's seat with Rankin in it was shot out of the plane. The seat was attached by a long cable to the inside of the jet. After the seat flew up into the air, it was pulled out from under Rankin.

The jet had been zooming along more than nine miles above the earth at about 500 miles an hour when Rankin ejected. When he hit the outside air, Rankin felt like a giant fist had punched his body. The force of the air ripped the glove off his left hand and the heavy curtain from in front of his face. It also tore the eye shield from his helmet.

And then Rankin felt the cold. In the plane, it had been 70 degrees above zero. But the air at nine miles above the earth is thin and icy. Outside the plane, it was 70 degrees *below* zero. That was a temperature drop of 140 degrees. To make matters worse, Rankin was dressed in a pilot's summer suit. After all, he hadn't planned to "leave" his jet while nine miles up. He felt as if he were being cut by hundreds of tiny icicles. He was on fire with pain. But moments later, his skin lost all feeling.

As Rankin tumbled through space, the pain from the change in air pressure started. The thin air made bubbles in Rankin's blood and pulled and twisted at him. His stomach swelled as though it had been pumped full of air. His eyes felt like they were being ripped from his head. Blood flowed from his eyes, his ears, his nose, and his mouth.

Even though he was in great pain, Rankin had made up his mind that he wouldn't pass out. His parachute was supposed to open by itself at 10,000 feet. That meant that he would fall free through space for about seven miles. But what if the parachute didn't open by itself? He wanted to be awake so he could pull the parachute-opening handle if he had to. Rankin also wanted to see what was happening. He wanted to be able to tell the Marine Corps doctors and generals what it was like to parachute from nine miles up. Nobody had parachuted from that far up before.

Finally, after seven or eight long minutes, the parachute opened. Although he hurt all over, Rankin felt like singing for joy. The air was thicker and warmer now. Best of all, his life-saving parachute was working fine. Rankin thought the worst was over, but the worst really hadn't begun yet.

Rankin shows how he fell through space for seven miles before his parachute opened.

All of a sudden, a powerful blast of air tossed Rankin upwards. Another blast pushed him down. Then he was tossed up again and then down again. Rankin had fallen into a thunderstorm. As he got closer to the center of the storm, the blasts of air got worse. Now Rankin was being tossed every which way—up, down, around, and sideways. It was too much for Rankin's stomach. He threw up time after time after time.

Then came the thunder. Rankin felt as though cannons were being shot off next to his ear. The thunder shook every bone in his body. Luckily, he still had his helmet on or his eardrums may have burst.

But the thunder wasn't all he had to put up with. Giant sheets of lightning flashed all around him. The lightning was so bright that Rankin could see it even with his eyes tightly closed. Meanwhile, the rains had started. The rain was so powerful that Rankin was afraid that he might become the first person to drown in the sky.

And then the rain changed to hail—huge, baseball-size chunks of ice. It was like being in a rain of rocks. Luckily, Rankin's helmet saved him once more. Without his helmet, the hail would almost certainly have cracked his skull. As it was, Rankin was badly bruised and cut.

Rankin was lucky, too, that the storm did not harm his parachute. When the hail hit, he was afraid it would rip holes in his chute. But the parachute was made of strong cloth.

Somehow during the storm, Rankin was able to glance at his watch. He was shocked by what he saw. He had been falling for some 30 minutes or more. But the trip down should have taken no more than 10 minutes. Rankin, it seems, was a prisoner of the storm. The upward blasts of air were keeping him from falling to the ground. He couldn't last much longer. Unless the storm "let him go" soon, he was a dead man.

At last, the clouds opened up and Rankin saw a flash of green below. After nearly 40 minutes, it looked like he was finally reaching the ground. But Rankin's troubles still weren't over.

A tree branch caught the top of Rankin's chute. He was slammed against the trunk and thrown to the ground. Dazed, Rankin couldn't move for a few seconds. Then soaked, frostbitten, bruised, cut, and covered with blood and mud, he limped to a nearby road.

When the drivers saw Rankin, they sped away. He looked like some kind of wild man from outer space.

Growing weaker, Rankin fell to his knees as still another car passed him. But then the car stopped and came back.

The car belonged to the Dunnings. One of the Dunning boys saw that the strange-looking man by the side of the road was wearing a pilot's helmet and suit. "That's a jet pilot! He's in trouble," the boy yelled.

When he got in the car and heard why the

Rankin had to spend some time in a hospital after his nine-mile jump.

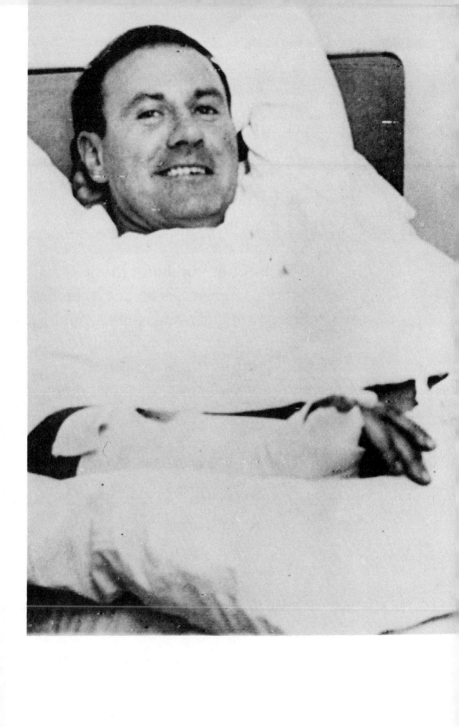

Dunnings stopped, Rankin gave his helmet to the boys. "Here, boys. Thanks," he said. "I owe you my life. There's your souvenir."

The Dunnings got Rankin to an ambulance in a hurry. Rankin had to spend some time in the hospital. But within a few weeks, he was OK.

People around the world were amazed by Bill Rankin. But Rankin didn't think he had done anything so great. As he put it, he had been trained to handle emergencies and he was just doing a job. But to people everywhere, falling into a thunderstorm and escaping from it alive are more than just doing a job.

7

THE LONG ESCAPE

It was a warm Friday afternoon in June of 1722. Taking it easy after a fishing trip, Philip Ashton watched as a boat carrying four men drew closer to his sailing ship, which was resting at anchor. The men looked harmless enough. They were coming from a large ship that had been sitting at anchor for several hours. But as soon as the small boat tied up to Ashton's sailing ship, the men whipped out swords and pistols and took over Ashton's ship.

As it turned out, the men worked for Ned Low, a well-known pirate. Philip and the five others aboard the sailing ship were taken aboard the large ship to meet Low.

Giving the prisoners a fierce look, Low asked, "Are any of you married men?" The prisoners were so surprised by the question that they didn't know what to say. Low grabbed Ashton and screamed in his face, "You dog, why don't you answer?"

Afraid for his life, Ashton, who happened to be single, answered that he wasn't married. Low calmed down when he heard Ashton's answer. Low did not like to take married men on his ship. He was afraid they would try to break away and return to their families.

The pirates tried to get Ashton to become one of them, but he refused. He also asked the pirates to set him free. The pirates wouldn't listen. One day a number of prisoners were put aboard a ship that was sailing to Boston. Ashton begged Low to let him go with them, but the pirate said no.

As the months passed, the pirates attacked dozens of ships. Ashton never took part in any of these raids. He hated pirates and their evil ways. He made up his mind to escape if he could, but there didn't seem to be any chance of that. Low would never let Ashton go ashore, not even with a guard. And Ashton was a poor swimmer, so he was afraid to try to swim to shore.

Then one day Ashton got his chance. Seven pirates were going ashore on a small island to fill up the ship's barrels with water. Low wasn't around. So Ashton went up to the pirate in charge. He explained that he hadn't set foot on land for many months. Ashton asked if he could go along and help fill the barrels. The pirate said he could.

When they landed, Ashton helped roll the barrels to a small stream. Then he headed for the woods. When the pirate in charge asked where he was going, Ashton answered that he wanted to get some coconuts. But as soon as he was out of sight, Ashton took off and hid in a clump of bushes deep in the forest.

When the barrels were full, the pirates

Ned Low, the pirate who captured Ashton, was almost killed in this storm.

74

called out for Ashton. When they got no reply, one man said, "The dog is lost in the woods and cannot find the way out again." The pirates began a search, but the woods were thick and they found no sign of Ashton.

After the pirates left, Ashton came out of hiding. He had gotten away from the pirates, but his life was still in danger. There were no people on the island. And Ashton had no food or tools. The only clothes he had were those he was wearing, which didn't include shoes.

In time, Ashton found plenty of water, fruit, and turtle eggs. He also built a small hut. But he really wished he had shoes and matches. The rough forest ground was cutting his feet to ribbons. And without matches he couldn't cook his food or warm himself when it got chilly.

One day as he was walking through the forest, Ashton spotted a funny-looking log. As he drew close, the "log" opened its huge jaws. It was a giant snake. Luckily, for Ashton, the snake didn't attack. But after that Ashton was careful not to step on any logs before taking a close look at them. The snake he had seen had been about 14 feet long and was as big around as his waist.

By hanging onto large bamboo poles and kicking with his feet, Ashton was able to make trips to a nearby island. Once a shark rammed him in the back just as he was floating into shore. The water was so shallow that the shark couldn't get at Ashton with its toothy jaws. But Ashton carried a bruise around for more than a week.

Another time a wild boar, which is a fierce pig, rushed at Ashton. Once again, luck was with Ashton. He grabbed a tree branch and swung himself upward. The boar ripped away part of Ashton's ragged pants, but Ashton was not hurt.

As the months passed, Ashton got lonelier and weaker. Then one day as he was looking out over the water, he spied a canoe with a man in it. The man, who was quite old, spoke English. He had come to the island to hide from the people of his village. The man told Ashton that the people wanted to punish him. But the man never explained why. The stranger had matches and meat with him. For the first time in nine months, Ashton had a hot meal. After three days, the man said he was going hunting on one of the other islands. He invited Ashton to come along. But Ashton was still feeling so weak that he said no.

About an hour after the man left in his canoe, a storm came up. Ashton never saw the man again. Ashton missed his company, but the food and matches the man left on the island helped keep Ashton alive.

Seven lonely months passed before Ashton got a chance to speak to another human being again. This time a party of 18 Englishmen came ashore. Spanish soldiers were after them. During much of the 1700s, Spain and England were at war with each other.

The Spanish soldiers never did find the men, but pirates did. About six months after the Englishmen landed on the island, pirates

Ashton's Memorial.

AN
HISTORY
OF THE
Strange Adventures,
AND
Signal Deliverances,
OF
Mr. *Philip Ashton,*

Who, after he had made his Escape from the
PIRATES, liv'd alone on a Desolate
Island for about Sixteen Months, &c.

WITH

A short Account of Mr. *Nicholas Merritt,*
who was taken at the same time.

To which is added

A *SERMON* on *Dan.* 3. 17.

By JOHN BARNARD, V. D. M.

We should not trust in our selves, but in God;
who delivered us from so great a Death, and doth
deliver; in whom we trust, that he will yet deliver us.
II. Cor. I. 9, 10.

BOSTON, N. E. Printed for *Samuel Gerrish,*
at his Shop in Corn-Hill, 1 7 2 5.

attacked the home the Englishmen had built there. Coming ashore, the pirates captured some of the men but later let most of them go. Ashton and three other men had escaped capture by hiding deep in the island's thick forest.

After the pirate attack, all but one of the men, John Symonds, left the island. Ashton wanted to go with them. But their boat was small and might not handle well in rough seas. The leader of the party talked Ashton into staying behind with John Symonds, who hoped to start a trading business.

Not long after that, three English ships stopped at the island to fill their water barrels. The commander of the three ships was Captain Dove. Dove lived in Salem, Massachusetts, which was an English colony at the time. Salem was just a few miles from where Ashton's parents lived. Captain Dove was only too happy to take Ashton home.

Ashton told about his escape from the pirates in a book printed in 1725.

On the evening of May 2, 1725, Philip Ashton knocked at the door of his father's house. It had been two years, ten months, and fifteen days since he had been captured by the pirates. He was greeted, he wrote later, "as one risen from the dead."

8

4,000 MILES TO FREEDOM

In 1939, Slavomir Rawicz, a lieutenant in the Polish army, was arrested by the Russians. He was said to be a spy. After spending nearly a year in jail, Slav was put on trial and was sentenced to 25 years of hard labor in Siberia. Siberia is a cold, rugged part of Russia. Most of Siberia is covered by snow during half of the year. But it wasn't the snow or the cold or the work that got to 25-year-old Slav. It was the idea that he would have to spend so much of his life there. "Twenty-five years," he would say to himself. "As long to go as I have already lived."

Rawicz was ordered to spend 25 years in a Russian prison camp like this one. Copyright G. D. Hackett, NY

Slav knew that somehow he would have to get away. But he figured he couldn't escape by himself. He would need the help of others, and he would need a plan.

Slav began hiding bits of bread, so he would have some food for his escape. He also began working on a plan, but none of his ideas seemed good enough. Then one day the prison camp's commander asked if anyone could fix his radio. Slav said he would give it a try. He didn't know that much about radios. But he hoped he might be able to get the radio going and learn something about what was happening in the outside world.

As he worked on the radio, Slav became friends with the commander and his wife. The commander's wife felt sorry for Slav. He became almost like a son to her. One day when the commander was not around, she talked to Slav about how a prisoner might escape. Going north was out of the question, she told him. The Arctic Ocean was north. She said it would be best to go south. Escaping prisoners could keep on going until they reached India. It was a journey of 4,000 miles. But no one would think that men on foot would try such a long, difficult trip. Going east or west would be much shorter, but that's where the guards would look.

Prisoners heading east or west were almost sure to be caught. She also told Slav that it would be best to sneak away on a snowy night. That way the tracks would be covered.

Slav took the hint. On a snowy night in April of 1941, Slav and six other prisoners—Sigmund Makowski, Anastazi Kolemenos, Anton Paluchowicz, Eugene Zaro, Zacharius Marchinkovas, and Smith, an American who never gave his first name—crept out of their prison hut. Then they searched until they found a low spot where the camp's barbed wire fence did not meet the ground. After digging through the snow which had piled up against the fence, they were able to slip under the fence. Finally, after climbing over two giant wooden fences and leaping over rolls of barbed wire, they were outside the camp. The men had just begun one of the longest, hardest escapes of all time.

Once outside the camp, the men dashed into the forests. They then slowed to a jog.

They didn't stop moving until nearly noon the next day. Even though they had gone south, they were still afraid of being caught. They wanted to put as many miles between themselves and the camp as they could. Besides, they wouldn't feel really free until they reached India. Getting to India meant crossing frozen fields, icy rivers, a desert, and rugged mountains. But the men wanted freedom badly. They were willing to pay the price.

Although it was freezing, the men did not dare light a fire. They would put up with the cold until they reached the Lena River, which was about a ten-day journey. There they would be far enough away to feel a little safer.

After a few weeks, the men ran out of food. The bread that Slav had hidden away was gone. The men had also eaten up the

On following pages: *The broken line shows the 4,000-mile trip the escapers made. From Camp 303, near the top of the map, they walked all the way to India, near bottom of the map.*

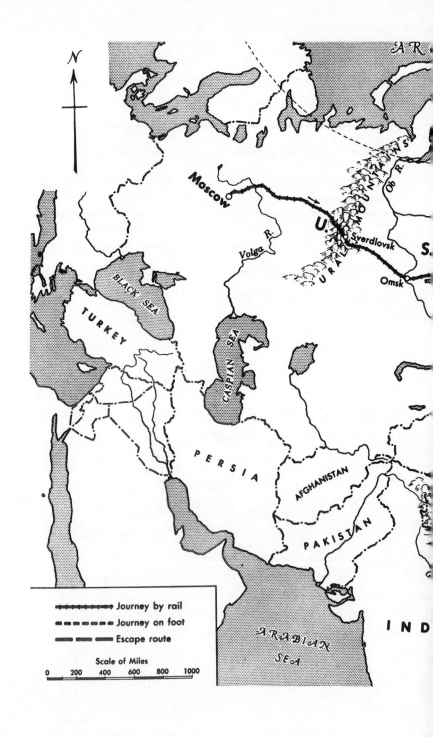

N

Moscow

Ob. R.

U.

Volga R.

Sverdlovsk

S.

Omsk

BLACK SEA

TURKEY

CASPIAN SEA

P E R S I A

AFGHANISTAN

PAKISTAN

I N D

A R A B I A N
SEA

AR

URAL MOUNTAINS

••••••••• Journey by rail

━ ━ ━ ━ Journey on foot

━━━ ━ ━━━ Escape route

Scale of Miles

0   200   400   600   800   1000

flour, bread, and barley that the commander's wife had slipped to them. If they were to stay alive, they would have to kill or trap some animals. One day they broke through a frozen stream and caught four fish. On another day, they killed a deer that had caught its antlers in a tree. The cooked deer meat was a delicious treat for the men. The deer's hide was used to make moccasins. The moccasins weren't very fancy, but they did the job.

Late one afternoon, Zaro, the lead man, suddenly threw his arm up. It was the danger signal. Zaro pointed toward some trees. Something was moving. Was it a man or an animal? No one could tell. But the creature seemed to be trying to hide.

Quickly but quietly, the men sneaked up on the creature's hiding place. Seeing boots sticking out from behind a bush, Slav grabbed them and pulled hard. The creature turned out to be a young girl. When questioned, she told how she escaped from a Russian prison camp. She had been put there by the Russians after her parents were killed by an angry mob. Her name was Kristina Polanska.

To the men, Kristina seemed like a daughter or a little sister. When she begged them to help her, they agreed to take her along.

After three months on the run, the band finally crossed over into Mongolia, a country between Russia and China. It had been a long difficult journey, but they were happy. The day before leaving Siberia they had found about 100 pounds of potatoes, which they put in their packs. "This is Russia's going-away gift," Slav thought to himself.

The group had gone some 1,200 miles. Still, their fear of being caught was strong. No matter how tired or cold or hungry they were, they forced themselves onward. They also stayed away from main roads and large cities. They didn't want to run into soldiers or police, who might start asking questions.

The Mongolian farmers and shepherds that they met were friendly people. The Mongols would bow low and give the strangers a hot meal and a place to stay. They would also give the escapers meat and cakes made of oats to take with them. The group, in return, would do some work for the farmer or shepherd. One day they helped two fishermen with their heavy nets. The fishermen gave them dozens of fish. The escapers dried and packed them away for their trip across the Gobi Desert.

Because it was summer, the Gobi was like a giant oven. Often the group traveled for days without water. And when the dried fish ran out, there was no food either. The blazing sun burned the escapers' skin and cracked their lips. They kept pebbles in their mouths to make a little spit and take their minds off their burning thirsts.

Once, when they were sure they were going to die, they found an oasis, a small spot of land where there was a pool of water and a few trees. "It is a miracle," Kristina sobbed when she spotted the water. Kristina and the others threw themselves on the ground and lapped up water like dogs. Then they cooled their blistered feet. Later, they found bones that still had meat on them. The bones had been left there just a day or two before by a caravan, a band of people on camels.

Some of the escapers wanted to stay at the oasis and wait for another caravan. But Slav thought they might have to wait for weeks. With the bones picked clean, there was no food left. He said they should go on. That may have been a mistake. Even today, Slav is not sure he did the right thing.

With just a day's supply of water, the group set out once more. On the fifth day, Kristina fell to the sand and passed out. After a short rest, she was up on her feet again. But her legs had begun to swell. She soon fell again. Slav and Kolemenos stayed at her side and helped her along. But after pushing through the sand, she fell once more. Now she was so weak she could not move. "Go on without me," she said to them. But the men wouldn't even think of going on without her. Kolemenos lifted

Kristina and carried her for some 200 yards. But the long day's march in the blazing sun had robbed Kolemenos of his strength. He could go no farther.

The group stopped there and rested for three hours. Then, once again, Kolemenos carried Kristina. He struggled through the sand with her for four straight hours. When his legs wanted to buckle, his heart made them move forward.

At last, Kristina whispered to Kolemenos, "Put me on the ground." On the ground, she looked at each of the men—these men who had become her family—and gave a little smile. Then her eyes closed. She was dead.

The men wept like babies. They blamed themselves for her death. Why had they brought her along, they asked, when they knew the trip would be so long and so hard? One man yelled at Slav. He said it was all Slav's fault. They should have stayed at the oasis.

Smith spoke up. "Gentlemen," he said, "it is no use blaming ourselves. I think she was happy with us." The men then buried Kristina.

The days passed. Still, there was no food or water. On the tenth day Makowski died. Two more days passed. The men were in serious trouble now. Without water and food, they would soon die. In the middle of the twelfth night, Slav told the men to get up and get moving. He knew that unless they found water very soon, they would all die. After hours of painful marching, they came aross a small mudhole. By pressing at the mud, they were able to squeeze water out of the hole.

Now they needed food. During the marches, the men had seen plenty of snakes, but they had never thought of eating them. Then Smith told them that the American Indians ate snakes. The men decided to give the snakes a try. The snakes didn't taste too bad. For the next few weeks, snake meat kept the men alive.

At last, the six men were out of the Gobi Desert. Even so, they were still many hundreds of miles from India. They still had to travel through the rest of Mongolia. And they had to journey through Tibet, a mountainous country whose sharp rocks would cut into their feet. And before reaching India, they had to cross the rugged Himalaya Mountains. The people of Tibet told them they would never make it across the mountains. But the men knew they would not feel free until they were in India. Their bodies were like robots. Once they got up in the morning, they just seemed to move ahead on their own.

One morning, though, Marchinkovas did not rise with the others. "Come on! Get up!" one of the men called. But Marchinkovas didn't move. His body had worn itself out. He had died during the night.

By March of 1942, after nearly a year on the run, the men could sense that they were near India and freedom. Just a few more tall mountains to cross. After climbing the last of the giant peaks, the men spotted two strange creatures. They were large and hairy

To get to India, the escapers had to climb over the Himalaya Mountains.

like apes, but they walked upright like men. They were seven to eight feet tall and reddish-brown in color. They seemed to have no fear. The beasts were on the slope that the men were climbing down. The men yelled at them, but they paid no attention. Smith thought the beasts, which some people now believe were Abominable Snowmen, might decide to come after them. So the men took another path.

The other path turned out to be dangerous. Anton Paluchowicz slipped through a crack in the mountain and fell thousands of feet to his death. The others were greatly saddened. As Smith put it, "All this way, to die so stupidly at the last."

A few days later, the men stumbled into India. They soon met up with a band of British soldiers. Because the soldiers spoke English, Smith talked to them. After hearing the story of the escape, the soldiers said they would help the men. Smith then turned to Slav and the others and said in Russian, "Gentlemen, we are safe."

The men were barely alive. But somehow they found the strength to laugh and sing and dance. They were free! What a wonderful feeling!

The soldiers gave the men food and clean clothes and took them to a hospital. After a month in the hospital, Slav joined up with some other Polish soldiers to fight in World War II.

Near the end of the war, he went to England to learn to be a pilot. While there, he met and married an English woman. Their life together was a rich and happy one. They raised five children and now have four grandchildren. Still, Slav sometimes has nightmares about his march to freedom. And he often wonders what happened to Smith, Zaro, and Kolemenos. He hasn't heard from them since they parted in India. He wishes them well. He hopes they have enjoyed their years of freedom as much as he has.

9

ONE CHANCE
IN A MILLION

The pilot, Captain del Rey, smiled to himself as the giant DC-8 touched down on the runway in Spain without so much as a bump. The smooth landing made up for the little bit of trouble during the takeoff from Cuba nine hours before. A red light on the panel had stayed on. The light signaled that the jet's wheels had not folded up into the wheel wells the way they were supposed to. But that problem was quickly solved. Del Rey simply let the wheels down and pulled them up again. The red light then went out.

Del Rey figured everything was OK. Later,

he would find out there was a reason why the light had gone on. And that reason was a very strange one.

Shortly after the DC-8 came to a stop, mechanics drove out to the runway to check it out. As they looked over the huge front wheels, something dropped from the jet's wheel wells and landed with a thud on the concrete. Seeing that it was a body, the mechanics cried out. A guard ran over to the body. "It's a man!" he yelled.

Actually, it wasn't a man. It was a teenager, 17-year-old Armando Socarras Ramírez from Cuba. His clothes were a sheet of ice. His body was frozen. Even his face was caked with ice. But Armando was alive. When the guard touched him, he moaned softly like a sick animal.

As he was getting out of the plane, del Rey heard the men yelling. He ran over to see what had happened. He was as surprised as the others. Then he suddenly knew why the red light had gone on.

The guard called an ambulance. The

young man was rushed to the nearest hospital. Before long, Armando came to and told of one of the most foolish but amazing escapes of all time.

Armando had hated life in Cuba. The country was run by a man by the name of Castro. Castro told the people how to live their lives. They had very little freedom and not much fun. At 16, Armando was sent to a school far from his home. He was supposed to be learning to be a welder. But he had to spend much of his time cutting sugar cane.

A dream was born in Armando's heart. He wanted to go the United States. He had an uncle who lived in New Jersey. He would go live with him and study to be an artist.

Still, getting to the United States seemed nearly hopeless. People were allowed to leave Cuba, but in the late 1960s only two planes flew to the U.S. each day. There was a list of 800,000 people waiting for seats on the planes. It would be years before Armando's turn came. Besides, once the government people knew you had signed up to leave, they began making life tough for you.

At a baseball game in Havana, Cuba's largest city, Armando met Jorge. Jorge, who was a year younger than Armando, also wanted to flee to the United States. One day Jorge and Armando went to the airport to watch the planes take off. Looking up, they saw a DC-8 heading out toward the Atlantic for its long flight to Madrid, Spain. Since its wheels were still down, they could see inside the large wheel wells. Suddenly the boys came up with a crazy idea. They would hide in the wheel wells and fly to Spain. From there, they could get to the United States fairly easily.

On June 3, 1969, Armando and Jorge hid in the grass near the end of the runway. A DC-8 taxied to the end of the runway, turned, and stopped for a few seconds. During those seconds, Jorge and Armando ran to the plane and climbed up the wheels into the wheel wells. Jorge climbed into the left wheel well. Armando went into the right one. They had put cotton in their ears to

Armando climbed into a wheel well of a DC-8 just before it took off.

soften the scream of the jet engines.

Grabbing onto pipes and cables, Armando pulled himself up into the wheel well and held on like glue as the giant jet sped down the runway. As the plane climbed into the sky, its huge wheels slowly folded into the wells. Armando squeezed himself as far into the wheel well as he could but the giant wheels kept on coming. Afraid that the wheels would crush him, Armando tried to hold them back with his feet. Finally, they stopped just inches away. "I'm safe," Armando thought to himself. But he wasn't.

Suddenly the wheels began moving away from Armando. The pilot was lowering them. Had Armando and Jorge been spotted? Was the pilot returning to the field to turn Jorge and him in? These questions raced around inside Armando's head. But he didn't have much time to think about them. The well's doors were open and the wheels were down. He held onto the cables with all his might as a cold blast of air nearly ripped him out of the well. Then the wheels started coming up again. In the meantime, Armando had spied a spot that had a little more room. Once again the wheels were pulled up and the well's doors closed.

As the plane climbed to 30,000 feet, the air became thin and cold. The temperature outside the plane dropped to 40 degrees below zero. Dressed only in light pants and a thin shirt, Armando began shivering. He also had pains in his ears. Feeling dizzy because of the thin air, Armando blacked out.

High above the Atlantic, the DC-8 sped toward Spain. Only once had Armando awakened. "It is terribly cold," he thought to himself. Then he blacked out once more. His chilled body became stiff. The warm air from his nose and mouth turned into water and froze.

Just a few miles from Madrid, the pilot lowered his wheels. Luck was with Armando. He had become twisted in the plane's cables and pipes and did not tumble out.

When the plane landed, luck was with Armando again. There wasn't even a thump when the jet's wheels met the runway. If the plane had bounced, even slightly, Armando could have been tossed onto the runway and killed.

Later, at the hospital, doctors couldn't say for sure what had kept Armando alive. They

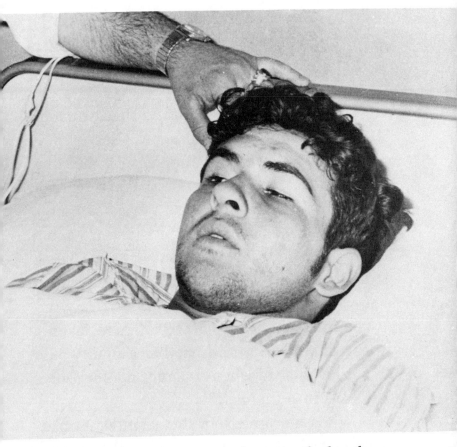

Nearly frozen to death, Armando was rushed to the hospital.

believed Armando's body may have gone into a deep sleep the way an animal's does when it hibernates for the winter. They

105

were sure that Armando's brain would be hurt and he would be sick for the rest of his life. But after a few days in the hospital, Armando was feeling fine.

No one was more surprised that Armando made it than Charles Glasgow. Glasgow was in charge of planning airplanes for the company that made DC-8s. He still can't understand why Armando wasn't crushed by the jet's wheels. He says there is enough room for a person in the well. But the well has so many cables and pipes that twisting yourself into the room that's left over is nearly impossible. As he explained, "There is only one chance in a million that a man would not be crushed when the huge double wheel folded into the well."

When he came to in the hospital, Armando asked about his friend Jorge. No one knew what happened to Jorge. He was not in the other wheel well. Now it is believed that Jorge fell down while trying to climb into the wheel well and was then put in jail for trying to escape.

After he got better, Armando was flown to New York, where he went to live with an uncle.

For a while, Armando was afraid that the Spanish goverment would return him to Cuba. "Please don't send me back to Cuba," he begged the government people. He told them that he wanted to go to the United States. "I have an uncle living in New Jersey and maybe he will help me," Armando explained.

Armando got his wish. A month later he flew to Kennedy Airport, which is not too far from New Jersey, to meet his uncle. This time he was on the inside of the plane.

When he got to Kennedy, Armando told why he had taken such a foolish chance. "There was no future in Cuba at all for me," he said to reporters. "I was looking for a new world and a new future. I would do it again."

INDEX

109

THOMAS G. GUNNING holds a doctorate in the Psychology of Reading from Temple University in Philadelphia and is currently an assistant professor in the Reading Department of Southern Connecticut State University. He has been a high school and junior high school English and reading teacher, an English department chairperson, and an elementary school reading consultant.

Dr. Gunning is the author of *Unexplained Mysteries*, a collection of nine strange but true happenings. He has also written six high-interest reading kits, a number of worktexts for students of all ages, and several articles on the teaching of reading. He has also edited a high-interest newspaper for schoolchildren.

Thomas G. Gunning makes his home in Newington, Connecticut, with his wife, Joan, and his children, Tom, Joy, Tim, and Faith.